QUICK & EASY PRESSURE CANNING RECIPES

The Ultimate and To the Point Super Easy Guide to Make Long Lasting Perfect Pressure Canned Foods in 30 Minutes or Less – Enjoy Tasty Canned Food Like Never Before.

BY

Nash Bobo

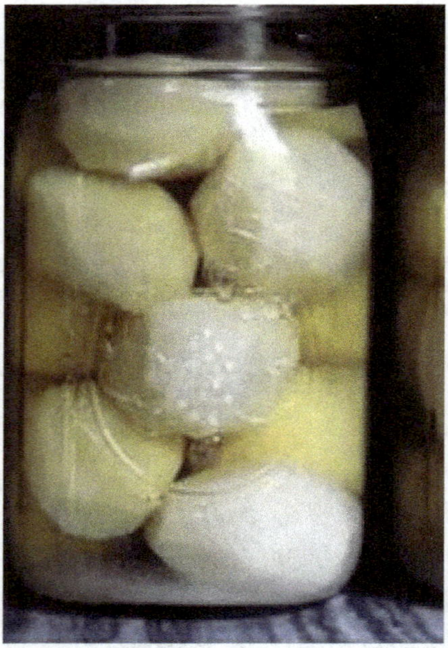

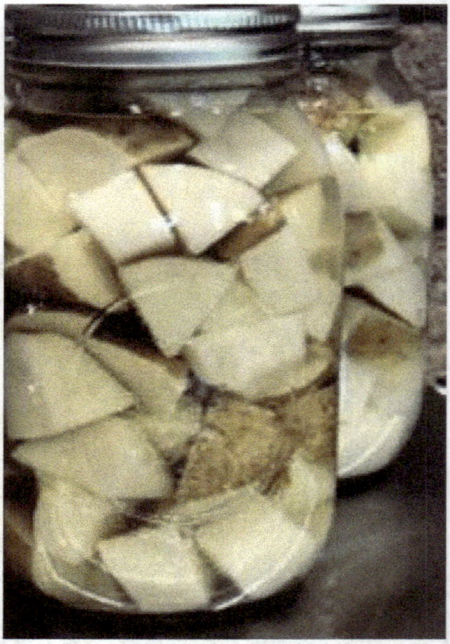

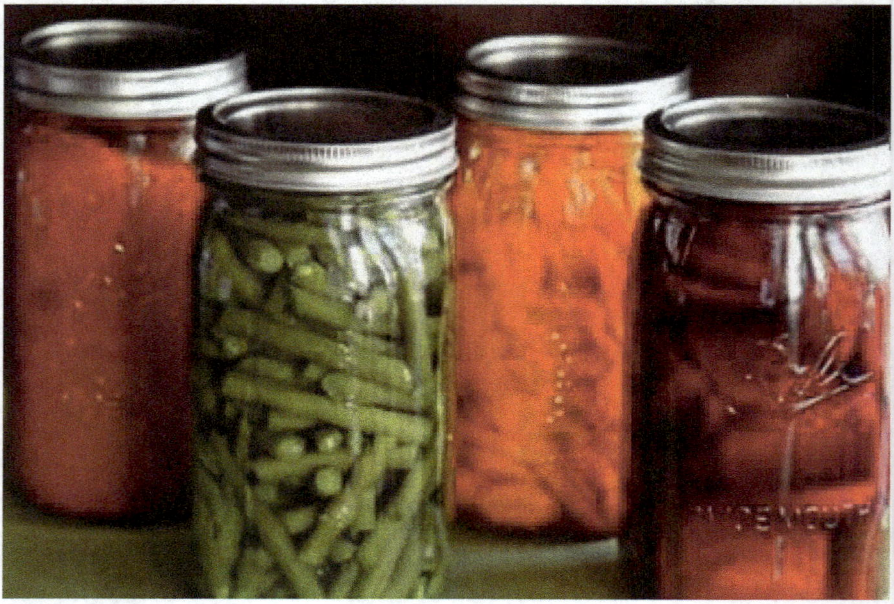

© Copyright 2021 - All rights reserved.

The content contained within this book may not be reproduced, duplicated or transmitted without direct written permission from the author or the publisher.

Under no circumstances will any blame or legal responsibility be held against the publisher, or author, for any damages, reparation, or monetary loss due to the information contained within this book. Either directly or indirectly.

Legal Notice:

This book is copyright protected. This book is only for personal use. You cannot amend, distribute, sell, use, quote or paraphrase any part, or the content within this book, without the consent of the author or publisher.

Disclaimer Notice:

Please note the information contained within this document is for educational and entertainment purposes only. All effort has been executed to present accurate, up to date, and reliable, complete information. No warranties of any kind are declared or implied. Readers acknowledge that the author is not engaging in the rendering of legal, financial, medical or professional advice. The content within this book has been derived from various sources.

Please consult a licensed professional before attempting any techniques outlined in this book. By reading this document, the reader agrees that under no circumstances is the author responsible for any losses, direct or indirect, which are incurred as a result of the use of information contained within this document, including, but not limited to, errors, omissions, or inaccuracies.

Table of Contents

Introduction ---------------------------------------7
1. Canning Turkey Stock ------------------------10
2. Canning Sausage--------------------------------17
3. Pressure Canning Pork Tenderloin ------------20
4. Spanish Salsa ----------------------------------22
5. Tomatillo Salsa --------------------------------25
6. Mexican Tomato Sauce -----------------------28
7. Eggplant Salsa ---------------------------------31
8. Tomatillo Salsa Verde--------------------------34
9. Chipotle Tomatillo Salsa ----------------------37
10. Salsa Ranchera-------------------------------40
11. Roasted Salsa Verde -------------------------44
12. Tomatillo Green Salsa -----------------------48
13. Pico De Gallo --------------------------------51
14. Salsa Roja ------------------------------------53
15. Roasted Tomato Guajillo Salsa--------------56
16. Green Tomato Salsa -------------------------59
17. Peach Salsa-----------------------------------61
18. Smoky Sour Cherry Tequila Salsa -----------65
19. Mild Salsa------------------------------------68

Conclusion --------------------------------------- 71

INTRODUCTION

TIPS FOR PREPARING DELICIOUS CANNED FOODS

Acquaint yourself with every one of the directions that accompanied your pressure canner. On the off chance that you don't have them, discover the producer's guidelines for that model on the web or contact the maker for help.

On the off chance that your canner has a dial measure, have it checked each year to guarantee its exactness. To discover where to get it tried, check your state or area's Cooperative Extension site or call your nearby Extension office. Or on the other hand contact your canner maker straightforwardly.

Plan to utilize new or moderately new Mason-style containers in sizes proper for your item. Save antiquated containers with wire bails and glass covers, fancy glass stockpiling containers, or reused pickle and peanut butter containers for different things.

Wash your containers in the dishwasher yet measure your canned merchandise just on a burner. It is by no means protected to can anything in a dishwasher, oven, or microwave.

Try not to adjust the extents of INGREDIENTS and don't add thickeners or different INGREDIENTS not indicated in the tried formula that you are using.

Adhere to the guidelines for filling the containers; leave the perfect measure of headspace and oppose the impulse to overload to get that last tad into the container. The predetermined head space permits space for the food inside to grow while heated and not meddle with the top's seal, making a solid vacuum as the container chills off.

Comply with the suggested times for venting and cooling the canner. Holding up the full time is fundamental to guarantee both the wellbeing of your completed item and your actual security (e.g., from steam consumes).

For best flavor and dietary benefit, eat what you've safeguarded inside a year or somewhere in the vicinity.

Can just the food varieties that you know you and your family will eat and enjoy—and you will enjoy the experience from starting to last chomp.

1. Canning turkey stock

Prep Time 1 hour Cook Time 25 minutes Total Time 1 hour 25 minutes Yield 1 Varies Calories 20 kcal

INGREDIENTS
- Turkey (corpse and bones)
- Water
- Salt (optional)

INSTRUCTIONS
1. Take turkey remains, clear all meat off it. (Tip: you can freeze meat in a baggie for adding to soup later.)
2. (Optional: Some individuals like to broil the cadaver for an hour or so now, for a more obscure, more extravagant tasting stock.)
3. EITHER : Put cadaver in pot with sufficient water to cover bones. Heat to the point of boiling, stew for 45 minutes. Or then again Put in pressure cooker. Add sufficient water to

cover bones. Cook for 30 minutes on high pressure (13 to 15 lbs for most North Americans. See Notes.) A couple cove leaves threw into either measure make a roused expansion.
4. Optionally, you can prepare with salt or a non-severe, non-obfuscating salt sub (like Herbamare), in any case, the plainer you leave the stock, the more adaptable it will be the point at which you go to utilize it.
5. Strain into a large bowl or tub; have a second go at taking a greater amount of the relaxed meat out it, add that to your sack of frozen meat, and put the confidence in refrigerator over night.
6. Toward the beginning of the day, scratch all the fat off the top; dispose of the fat and any additional sound leaves.
7. Reheat the stock to bubbling in a pot or a microwave (mind the flood while eliminating from microwave.)
8. Empty hot into half-liter (1 US half quart) jars or 1 liter (US quart) jars.
9. Leave 3 cm (1 inch) headspace.
10. Wipe jar edges.
11. Put tops on, put in pressure canner.
12. Preparing pressure: 10 lbs (69 kPa) weighted check, 11 lbs (76 kpa) dial measure (change pressure for your height when more than 300 meters/1000 feet.)
13. Handling time: half-liter (1 US half quart) jars for 20 minutes. Or then again 1 liter (1 US quart) jars for 25 minutes.
14. Home/Meat/Canning turkey stock

15. CANNING TURKEY STOCK
16. Documented Under: Meat, Seasonal Winter
17. Labeled With: Meat, Turkey
18. Leap to Recipe Print Recipe
19. Canning turkey stock001
20. Home canned turkey stock is a pleasure to add to risottos, sauces and sauces; it adds a brilliant profundity of flavor just as supplements. You may wish to broil the bones first for a considerably more profound flavor.

21. Here we are working with a recipe from the USDA Complete Guide.
22. See additionally: Canning Turkey, Canning Chicken Stock.
23. Substance stow away
24. THE RECIPE
25. Jar size decisions: Either half-liter (1 US half quart) OR 1 liter (1 US quart)
26. Handling technique: pressure canning as it were
27. Yield: differs
28. Headspace: 3 cm (1 inch)
29. Handling pressure: 10 lbs (69 kPa) weighted measure, 11 lbs (76 kpa) dial check (change pressure for your elevation when more than 300 meters/1000 feet.)
30. Handling time: Half-liters (pints) 20 minutes; liters (quarts) 25 minutes.
31. 5 from 1 vote
32. Print
33. Canning turkey stock

34. This is a recipe for without fat turkey stock. All the flavor without the calories, oil and the salt over-burden.
35. Course Main Course
36. Cooking American
37. Catchphrase Turkey
38. Planning Time 60 minutes
39. Cook Time 25 minutes
40. Complete Time 1 hour 25 minutes
41. Yield 1 Varies
42. Calories 20 kcal
43. INGREDIENTS
44. turkey (body and bones)
45. water
46. salt (optional)
47. Guidelines
48. Take turkey cadaver, clear all meat off it. (Tip: you can freeze meat in a baggie for adding to soup later.)
49. (Optional: Some individuals like to cook the cadaver for an hour or so now, for a more obscure, more extravagant tasting stock.)
50. EITHER : Put corpse in pot with sufficient water to cover bones. Heat to the point of boiling, stew for 45 minutes. Or then again Put in pressure cooker. Add sufficient water to cover bones. Cook for 30 minutes on high pressure (13 to 15 lbs for most North Americans. See Notes.) A couple inlet leaves threw into either measure make a roused expansion. Optionally, you can prepare with salt or a non-unpleasant, non-obfuscating salt sub (like Herbamare), however, the plainer you leave the stock, the

more adaptable it will be the point at which you go to utilize it. –
51. Strain into a large bowl or tub; have a second go at taking a greater amount of the slackened meat out it, add that to your pack of frozen meat, and put the confidence in ice chest over night.
52. In the first part of the day, scratch all the fat off the top; dispose of the fat and any additional sound leaves.
53. Reheat the stock to bubbling in a pot or a microwave (mind the flood while eliminating from microwave.)
54. Empty hot into half-liter (1 US half quart) jars or 1 liter (US quart) jars.
55. Leave 3 cm (1 inch) headspace.
56. Wipe jar edges.
57. Put covers on, put in pressure canner.
58. Handling pressure: 10 lbs (69 kPa) weighted measure, 11 lbs (76 kpa) dial check (change pressure for your elevation when more than 300 meters/1000 feet.)
59. Handling time: half-liter (1 US half quart) jars for 20 minutes. Or on the other hand 1 liter (1 US quart) jars for 25 minutes.
60. Instructions to pressure can.
61. At the point when pressure canning, you should change the pressure for your elevation.
62. For salt substitute, we utilized Herbamare Sodium-Free as it is non-harsh and non-obfuscating in canning.
63. NOTES
64. You may see a few group saying they stew or heat up their bones for stock for 5 or 6 hours.

This is a hopeless cause, as pressure cooking them for 30 minutes will yield similar outcomes, with a small part of the energy utilization. Should you decide to bubble, notice that the USDA proposes that 45 minutes is totally sufficient. Any time past that has zero advantage to show for it.

65. For pressure cooking (note, not pressure canning), HIGH PRESSURE approaches 13 to 15 lbs, or 90 to 100 kilopascals, or .9 to 1 bar. [1] The pressure cooking season of 30 minutes for poultry stock,. Note: in the event that you are using an electric pressure cooker to make the stock in, like an Instant Pot, she encourages expanding the opportunity to 33 to 35 minutes.
66. Pressure cooking utilizes less energy and concentrates more flavor and gelatin from the bones, bringing about a superior quality stock.
67. Most importantly, kindly keep clear the contrast between pressure cooking the stock to save energy and produce an unrivaled stock, and afterward pressure canning it later to safeguard it.
68. At the point when you first dish the turkey, deglaze the broiling skillet with a modest quantity of bubbling water from a pot. Empty that into a tub and let sit for the time being in cooler, skim fat off the following day. This will typically be a stunning jam like stock. Add that to the bunch of stock you are making. On the off chance that you do broil the turkey cadaver, deglaze that cooking dish along these lines, as well.

69. Broiling the turkey remains can bring about an awesome profound rich flavor yet additionally brings about a very dull stock, ordinarily (photographs show contrast in stocks from cooked and unroasted bodies.)
70. Wellbeing tip: After you have a plate of meat you have taken out a turkey body, consistently require a moment to feel cautiously through that meat with your fingers, squeezing everything, feeling for little bones. Be especially aware of misleading level bones from turkey legs.
71. An inlet leaf or two while you are bubbling or pressure cooking the bones will hoist your stock.
72. You could add a touch of salt or non-unpleasant, non-blurring salt sub per jar, yet it very well may be contended that it's simply better to can it with no guarantees, at that point do season changes when you go to utilize it in something. Salt adds zero towards the wellbeing of this recipe; it's simply a flavoring here. The security is the pressure canning measure.

2. Canning sausage

Prep Time 30 minutes Cook Time 1 hour 30 minutes Total Time 2 hours Yield 1 varies Calories 304 kcal

INGREDIENTS
- Sausage
- Water

INSTRUCTIONS
1. Slice interface sausage into 3 to 10 cm (1 to 4 inch) pieces. Or on the other hand
2. In the event that it's free sausage meat you have, shape into 10 cm (4 inch) or more modest patties or balls.
3. Brown gently in griddle.
4. Channel off abundance fat (it may go malodorous away.)
5. Pack hot into ½ liter (US half quart) jars or 1 liter (US quart) jars.
6. Leave 3 cm (1 inch) headspace.

7. Load up with bubbling water, bubbling stock or bubbling tomato juice, leaving 3 cm (1 inch) headspace.
8. Debubble, change headspace.
9. Wipe jar edges.
10. Put tops on.

11. Preparing pressure: 10 lbs (69 kPa) weighted check, 11 lbs (76 kpa) dial measure (change pressure for your height when more than 300 meters/1000 feet.)
12. Preparing time: ½ liter (US half quart) jars for 75 minutes OR 1 liter (US quart) jars for an hour and a half.
13. RECIPE NOTES
14. Shower container delicately with cooking splash or oil when you begin to brown the sausages; from that point onward, they should deliver sufficient fat all alone. In the event that it's a very lean sausage, however, you may need to rehash utilizations of the cooking shower.
15. The canning proposal directions have the assumption that the sausage pieces or patties will be going hot into the jar. A deferral of a couple of moments would be fine while they are being depleted of oil; simply not stone virus.
16. Honestly, in the event that you are canning "interface sausage", it is fine to leave the "packaging" on.
17. Regardless of what you read on the Internet, don't do a crude pack. The meat would cluster

together and cause heat infiltration issues. Also, don't do a dry pack. It is profoundly hazardous; the heat infiltration and developments in the jar with simply air would be altogether different based on what was tried with a fluid to guarantee your security. You should brown the meat to forestall clustering, and you should have a canning fluid in the jar. Something else, freeze your sausage (the quality is better, at any rate.

3. Pressure canning pork tenderloin

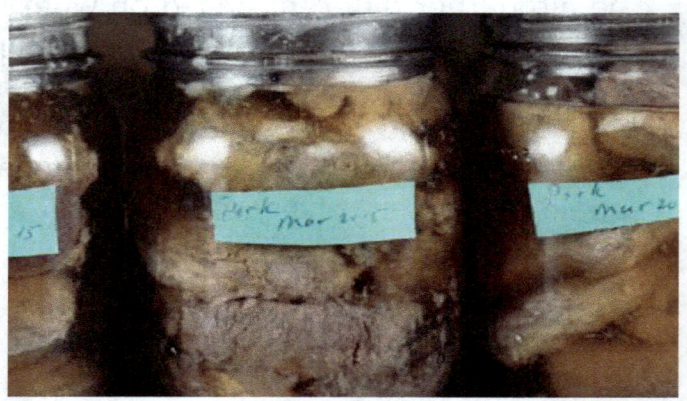

Prep Time 1 hour Cook Time 1 hour 30 minutes Total Time 2 hours 30 minutes Yield 1 varies Calories 143 kcal

INGREDIENTS
- Pork tenderloin
- Water

INSTRUCTIONS
1. Cut meat into 3D squares or strips.
2. Splash a skillet with cooking shower or heat a limited quantity of fat or oil in it.
3. Brown meat in the skillet in bunches; move browned meat to a covered bowl or pot to keep hot.
4. Pack meat into half-liter (1 US half quart) OR 1 liter (1 US quart) jars.
5. Leave 3 cm (1 inch) headspace.
6. Optional: a touch of salt or non-unpleasant, non-obfuscating salt sub per jar.

7. Top jars up with a bubbling fluid (water from a pot, stock, or tomato juice heated to the point of boiling) keeping 3 cm (1 inch) headspace.
8. Dabble; change headspace.
9. Wipe jar edges.
10. Put covers on.
11. Handling pressure: 10 lbs (69 kPa) weighted measure, 11 lbs (76 kpa) dial check (change pressure for your height when more than 300 meters/1000 feet.)
12. Handling time: half-liter (US half quart) jars for 75 minutes OR 1 liter (US quart) jars for an hour and a half.
13. Tips:
14. in the event that you have a ton of meat to brown, spread it out in cooking container/plate and burn in a hot oven until brown outwardly yet uncommon within.
15. You may utilize a microwave to heat to the point of boiling any canning fluid like stock or tomato juice — be cautious when moving heated fluid from a microwave as it can flood.

4. Spanish Salsa

Prep Time 1 hour 15 minutes Cook Time 1 hour Total Time 2 hours 15 minutes Yield 4 x half-litre (US pint) jars Calories 9 kcal

INGREDIENTS
- 400 g simmered red pepper (1 ¾ cups/14 oz. Estimations after prep.)
- 1.5 kg tomato (stripped, cultivated, chopped. 8 cups/3 ⅓ lbs. Estimations after prep.)
- 350 g onion (medium-chopped 2 ½ cups/12 oz)
- 4 New Mexico chiles (dried)
- 2 cloves garlic (stripped and minced)
- 1 twig rosemary (new)
- 100 ml sherry vinegar 5% or higher (⅓ cup + 1 tablespoon/3 oz)
- 1 tablespoon salt (or non-harsh, non-obfuscating salt sub)
- 1 tablespoon sugar
- 1 ½ teaspoons smoked paprika
- ½ teaspoon ground cumin
- 2 tablespoons lemon juice (new)

INSTRUCTIONS
1. Prep the cooked peppers (see Reference underneath); put in a large pan.
2. Prep the tomatoes (see Reference underneath); add to pot.
3. Prep the onion; add to pot.
4. Toast the chiles in an ungreased dish until they obscure a piece. At that point eliminate, let cool. At the point when cool, eliminate stems and seeds, at that point granulate to a powder. Add to pot.
5. Add to pot all INGREDIENTS down to and including the cumin (however NOT the lemon juice.)
6. Put pot over medium-high heat and heat to the point of boiling, mixing as often as possible.
7. Diminish heat to medium.
8. Let stew uncovered for around 30 to 45 minutes or until not, at this point watery. Mix every now and again. (Remember salsas are consistently thicker when they cool.)
9. Eliminate branch of rosemary if using.
10. Add lemon juice, let blend stew for an additional 2 minutes.
11. Spoon hot salsa into hot jars.
12. Leave 2 cm (½ inch) headspace.
13. Debubble, change headspace.
14. Wipe jar edges.
15. Put covers on.
16. Cycle in a water shower or steam canner.
17. Interaction jars for 20 minutes; increment time on a case by case basis for your height.
18. RECIPE NOTES

19. You need to purchase around 700 g (1 ½ lbs) of new pepper to wind up with the ideal amount in the wake of simmering
20. You need about 3.5 kg (7.7 lbs) of new tomato to wind up with the ideal amount after prep.
21. They recommend using sweet or Spanish onion.
22. New Mexico chiles (also known as green chiles) are known for gentle heat however loads of flavor. Rather than them, you can utilize 4 guajillo chiles, or 4 teaspoons ancho powder, or 4 teaspoons of a more blazing style paprika like Hungarian.
23. In the event that you don't have new rosemary, preclude, or utilize 1 teaspoon dried ground (not the dried "twigs" kind except if you put them in a piece of cheesecloth that can be taken out and disposed of.)
24. Rather than new lemon juice, you can utilize packaged. The lemon juice is there to spruce up the taste, so the typical necessity for rigorously packaged doesn't make a difference.
25. Allow jars to represent in any event seven days prior to testing.
26. Tip! You could prepare the broiled red pepper the other day and simply refrigerate it short-term, to save time on canning day,

5. Tomatillo Salsa

Prep Time 40 minutes Cook Time 1 hour 10 minutes Total Time 1 hour 50 minutes Yield 8 x quarter-litre (½ US pint) jars Calories 11 kcal

INGREDIENTS
- 4 green peppers (sweet, like chime)
- 6 jalapeno peppers
- 1 kg tomatillos new, chopped. 6 cups/2 lbs. Estimated after prep)
- 350 g onion (chopped, white. 2 cups/¾ lb. Estimated after prep)
- 4 cloves garlic
- 150 ml white wine vinegar (5% or higher. ⅔ cup/5 oz)
- 1 tablespoon salt (OR non-severe, non-obfuscating salt sub)
- 1 teaspoon ground coriander
- 1 teaspoon ground cumin
- ¼ teaspoon ground black pepper
- 50 g coriander (also known as cilantro. Finely chopped new. About ¾ cup pressed. 2 oz.)
- 10 g parsley (new, finely chopped. ½ cup/.5 oz)

- 4 tablespoons lime juice (60 ml/2 oz)

INSTRUCTIONS
1. Begin heating oven to 240 C/475 F.
2. Get a large, rimmed preparing sheet and line it with tin foil. Try not to oil or splash. Put away.
3. Wash, stem and seed every one of the peppers.
4. Spot on preparing sheet cut side down.
5. Prepare until scorched - around 30 minutes.
6. In the interim, eliminate and dispose of the husks from the tomatillos. Wash well.
7. Slash the tomatillos, add to large pot.
8. Add the INGREDIENTS down to and including the black pepper to the pot.
9. Wash and hack the cilantro and the parsley, put away.
10. At the point when peppers are done, eliminate from oven, and let cool until peppers can be securely taken care of.
11. Cleave peppers and add to pot.
12. Turn burner heat on, and heat pot to the point of boiling, covered.
13. At that point bring down the heat to medium, and stew for 5 minutes.
14. Uncover the pot, and let stew until it thickens with a ton of the water driven off - around 30 minutes.
15. Add cilantro, parsley, lime juice. Mix.
16. Stew 3 additional minutes to heat through.
17. Spoon hot salsa into hot jars.
18. Leave 2 cm (½ inch) headspace.
19. Debubble, change headspace.
20. Wipe jar edges.

21. Put tops on.
22. Interaction in a water shower or steam canner.
23. Cycle jars for 20 minutes; increment time on a case by case basis for your elevation
24. RECIPE NOTES
25. Rather than white wine vinegar, you could simply utilize white vinegar (5% or higher);
26. Rather than 4 cloves of garlic, you can utilize 2 teaspoons of minced garlic from a without oil container of minced garlic.

6. Mexican Tomato Sauce

Prep Time 45 minutes Cook Time 2 hours Total Time 2 hours 45 minutes

INGREDIENTS
- 250 ml tomato juice (1 cup/8 oz)
- 300 g onion washed, stripped and chopped (2 cups/10 oz/2 large)
- 2 kg tomatoes (paste-type. 4 ½ lbs/around 15 large)
- 75 ml lime juice (packaged. ⅓ cup/3 oz)
- 2 teaspoons salt OR non-severe, non-blurring salt sub
- 1 teaspoon cumin (optional)
- Chipotle chiles (1 or 2 in adobo sauce. Optional.)
- 6 cloves garlic washed, stripped and chopped
- 30 g cilantro (chopped. Also known as new coriander. ¼ cup/1 oz)

INSTRUCTIONS

1. Put every one of the INGREDIENTS from the tomato squeeze down to and remembering the garlic for a pot that is in any event 6 liters/quarts huge.
2. Heat to the point of boiling, at that point lower to a stew, cover and let stew for around 45 minutes or until onion is delicate. Mix occasionally to guarantee there is no singing.
3. Put combination through a food factory, using fine screen.
4. Put sauce in pot or dish with an extremely wide surface territory to speed vanishing - Ball recommends even a wide skillet.
5. Heat to the point of boiling, at that point lessen to a stew and let stew until it arrives at a consistency you are content with. To get the 4 jars that Ball says the recipe yields, that ought to be around 30 minutes, until it's the consistency of a slim ketchup.
6. Wash and hack cilantro, mix in.
7. Change taste whenever wanted with dry flavors.
8. Jar size: half-liter/half quart or more modest.
9. Put hot sauce into heated jars.
10. Leave 2 cm (½ inch) headspace.
11. Debubble, change headspace.
12. Wipe jar edges.
13. Put covers on.
14. Cycle in a water shower canner or steam canner.
15. Cycle jars for 40 minutes. Increment time depending on the situation for your elevation.
16. RECIPE NOTES

17. For the tomatoes, you can utilize Roma or any plum-type tomato.
18. Rather than 6 cloves of garlic, you can utilize 3 teaspoons of minced garlic from a without oil container of minced garlic.
19. On the off chance that you don't have a food factory, you can handle the combination in a food processor, at that point press through a strainer.
20. Elective flavors: chipotle powder, bean stew powder, teaspoon or two of dry unadulterated cocoa powder for a mole-type taste, scarcely any drops fluid smoke, dried chile pieces.
21. Rather than purchasing an entire container of adobo peppers just to utilize a couple of, a decent option may be the chipotle powder referenced above, or a couple of drops of a hot sauce, for example, Tabasco alongside a couple of drops of fluid smoke.
22. Rather than the new cilantro, you could attempt a tablespoon or two of dried parsley.
23. The weight appeared on the cilantro is wet, in the wake of washing.
24. Need to freeze this as opposed to canning? Freeze in straight-sided compartments with around 1 inch (3 cm) headspace.

7. Eggplant Salsa

Prep Time 1 hour 15 minutes Cook Time 1 hour Total Time 2 hours 15 minutes Yield 4 half-litre jars Calories 10 kcal

INGREDIENTS
- 500 g eggplant (stripped, diced eggplant. 8 cups/1 ¼ lbs. Estimated after prep)
- 1 tablespoon salt
- 400 g red pepper (broiled, stripped. 2 cups/14 oz. Estimated after prep)
- 1.2 kg tomato (stripped, cultivated, chopped. 5 cups/2.5 lbs. Estimated after prep.)
- 3 cloves garlic
- 250 g onion (finely chopped. 1 ½ cups/8 oz. Estimated after prep)
- 1 ½ teaspoons fennel seeds
- 1 ½ teaspoons chile chips
- 125 ml red wine vinegar (5% or higher. ½ cup/4 oz)
- 1 ½ teaspoons oregano (dried)
- 1 teaspoon sugar
- ¼ teaspoon ground black pepper

INSTRUCTIONS
1. Wash eggplant and strip.
2. Dice eggplant to 1 cm (½ inch) pieces.
3. Put in a bowl, blend in with 2 teaspoons of the salt.
4. Cover, let represent 2 hours, throw once in a while as the fluid is drawn out of the eggplant.
5. In the interim, prep (or buy) the broiled red pepper; put away.
6. Prep the tomatoes; put away.
7. Press out any overabundance dampness staying in eggplant; dispose of fluid.
8. Put eggplant away.
9. Wash, strip and mince the garlic; put away.
10. Wash, strip, hack the onion finely, measure; put away.
11. Put a large pot over medium heat. Heat dry briefly.
12. Add the fennel seed and hot pepper chips, toast briefly or until smell is delivered.
13. Add saved eggplant, broiled pepper, tomato, garlic, onion.
14. Add every leftover fixing, mix.
15. Cover dish, heat container to the point of boiling, at that point decrease heat to medium.
16. Stew covered for 10 minutes.
17. Uncover, at that point stew for around an additional 15 minutes, or until combination has thickened somewhat (not all that much - recall, it will thicken all the more once cooled.) Stir intermittently.
18. Spoon hot salsa into hot jars.
19. Leave 2 cm (½ inch) headspace.

20. Debubble, change headspace.
21. Wipe jar edges.
22. Put covers on.
23. Cycle in a water shower or steam canner.
24. Cycle jars for 20 minutes; increment time depending on the situation for your height.
25. RECIPE NOTES
26. Utilize red shepherd peppers when they are in season, and customary red chime peppers when they are definitely not.
27. You need to begin with 700 g/1.5 lbs of unpeeled eggplant. Around 2 medium.
28. You need to begin with around 2 kg (5 lbs) of tomatoes
29. Tip! You could prepare the broiled red pepper the other day and simply refrigerate it short-term, to save time on canning day.
30. Tip! Not an enthusiast of fennel seed? It's only there as a flavoring and has no wellbeing job. You can simply overlook, or utilize a similar measure of another dry zest seed that you think may work flavor-wise.

8. Tomatillo Salsa Verde

Prep Time 1 hour Cook Time 1 hour Total Time 2 hours Yield 4 quarter-litre jars Calories 26 kcal

INGREDIENTS
- 900 g tomatillos (chopped. 5.5 cups/2 lbs, estimated after prep)
- 175 g onion (chopped . 1 cup/6 oz, estimated after prep)
- 150 g chile peppers (chopped new hot green. 1 cup/5 oz, estimated after prep)
- 4 cloves garlic
- 2 tablespoons coriander (otherwise known as cilantro. New. Finely chopped (estimated after prep)
- 2 teaspoons ground cumin
- ½ teaspoon salt (OR non-harsh, non-blurring salt sub)
- ½ teaspoon chile pieces
- 250 ml white vinegar (5% or higher. 1 cup/8 oz)
- 4 tablespoons lime juice (50 ml/2 oz)

INSTRUCTIONS
1. Husk tomatillos, wash tenacity off them, hack, add to a large pot.
2. Wash onion, strip, cleave, add to pot.
3. Wash pepper, eliminate seeds, cleave, add to pot.
4. Strip and mince garlic, add to pot.
5. Wash and hack the new coriander (cilantro), add to pot.
6. Add all excess INGREDIENTS to pot.
7. Heat to the point of boiling, mixing regularly.
8. Lower to a solid stew, and let stew uncovered for 10 minutes.
9. Spoon hot salsa into hot jars.
10. Leave 2 cm (½ inch) headspace.
11. Debubble, change headspace.
12. Wipe jar edges.
13. Put tops on.
14. Cycle in a water shower or steam canner.
15. Handled 15 minutes for quarter-liter (half-16 ounces) jars; 20 minutes for half-liters
16. RECIPE NOTES
17. The beat button on a food processor deals with the cleaving.
18. For the hot pepper, we utilized 2 new green poblanos and one new green jalapeno for a to some degree hot taste. For more smoking, you could utilize all jalapeno. By new, we mean instead of dried.
19. In the event that you couldn't care less about keeping the salsa all green, you may utilize any shade of new chile peppers.

20. Rather than 4 cloves of garlic, you can utilize 2 teaspoons of minced garlic from a sans oil container of minced garlic.

9. Chipotle Tomatillo Salsa

Prep Time 45 minutes Cook Time 1 hour 30 minutes Total Time 2 hours 15 minutes

INGREDIENTS
- 1 kg tomatillos (2 lbs)
- 1 onion (little)
- 4 cloves garlic
- 4 tablespoons lime juice (new. 60 ml/2 oz)
- ½ teaspoon salt (OR non-unpleasant, non-obfuscating salt sub)
- 3 to 4 chipotle chiles (canned)

INSTRUCTIONS
1. Begin heating oven to 220 C/425 F.
2. Get a large, rimmed preparing sheet and line it with tin foil. Try not to oil or shower. Put away.
3. Eliminate and dispose of the husks from the tomatillos. Wash well.

4. Orchestrate tomatillos on heating sheet stem side down.
5. Wash the onion, leave unpeeled. Cut into equal parts. Spot on preparing sheet cut side down.
6. Leave garlic unpeeled. Add to preparing sheet.
7. Prepare until tomatillos and onion are delicate and start to burn - around 20 minutes.
8. Eliminate from oven, and let cool until onion can be securely dealt with.
9. Put tomatillos in a food processor bowl.
10. Strip the onion, dispose of the strip, add onion to food processor.
11. Cut warns garlic cloves, crush garlic out into food processor, dispose of the garlic strip.
12. Add all excess INGREDIENTS to food processor.
13. Wonder until smooth; how smooth is down to you yet you likely need to leave a touch of surface at any rate in it.
14. Move to a pot, heat to the point of boiling on the oven.
15. Scoop hot salsa into hot jars.
16. Leave 2 cm (½ inch) headspace.
17. Debubble, change headspace.
18. Wipe jar edges.
19. Put tops on.
20. Interaction in a water shower or steam canner.
21. Cycle jars for 25 minutes; increment time depending on the situation for your height.
22. RECIPE NOTES
23. 1 little onion = 40 g to 70 g (1.5 oz to 2.5 oz)
24. Rather than 4 cloves of garlic, you can utilize 2 teaspoons of minced garlic from a sans oil

container of minced garlic. Add it later as opposed to cooking it.

25. Rather than new lime juice, you can utilize packaged. In the case of using new, you'll need 2 to 3 key limes.
26. Make your limes yield more squeeze by destroying them in the microwave, just until they feel warm outwardly. Around 30 seconds in a 1200 watt microwave; your mileage will differ. In any case, you will get much more squeeze out of your limes (and lemons) with this stunt.
27. For the chiplote peppers, they are after the ones that come in little tins in adobo sauce. You will not need the entire tin; you can freeze the rest for another utilization later.

10. Salsa Ranchera

Prep Time 45 minutes Cook Time 2 hours Total Time 2 hours 45 minutes Yield 4 half-litre jars (US pint) Calories 56 kcal

INGREDIENTS
- 1.5 kg plum tomatoes (3 lbs. Weight before prep.)
- 350 g jalapeno peppers (¾ lb. Weight before prep.)
- 4 cloves garlic
- 1 onion (medium-sized. Around 100 g/3 oz)
- 75 ml lime juice (new. ⅓ cup/2.5 oz. Around 3 to 4 key limes)
- 30 g coriander (otherwise known as cilantro. New. ½ cup finely chopped. 1 oz)
- 2 teaspoons salt (OR non-unpleasant, non-blurring salt sub)

INSTRUCTIONS
1. Preheat oven to 225 C/425 F.
2. Line a rimmed heating sheet with tin foil.

3. Wash and center the tomatoes, put on heating sheet.
4. Wash peppers, cut down the middle, stem, place cut side down on heating sheet. (You can likewise eliminate a few or the entirety of the seeds where a ton of the heat is in the event that you wish.)
5. Strip garlic, put on preparing sheet
6. Strip onion, cut into thick (2 cm/½ inch) cuts, add to preparing sheet.
7. Put plate in oven, prepare until garlic cloves are delicate - around 20 minutes.
8. Eliminate garlic cloves, hack, put in a large pot.
9. Set plate back in oven, and heat until onion is delicate - about an additional 15 minutes. Peppers ought to be beginning to scorch a piece and the pepper skins ought to get wrinkled.
10. Eliminate plate from oven.
11. Allow plate additionally to stand 15 minutes to cool a piece.
12. Then, squeeze the limes. Put squeeze away.
13. Wash and finely cleave the new coriander; put away.
14. Take skin off tomatoes, coarsely hack, add to pot where garlic is.
15. Coarsely hack onion, add to pot.
16. Cleave garlic, add to pot.
17. Strip peppers. Dispose of skin.
18. Finely hack the peppers, add to pot.
19. Heat pot to the point of boiling, mixing much of the time.

20. Decrease heat, and let stew uncovered 2 minutes.
21. Mix in the readied lime juice, new coriander and salt.
22. Scoop hot sauce into heated jars, leaving 2 cm (½ inch) headspace.
23. Debubble, change headspace.
24. Wipe jar edges.
25. Put tops on.
26. Interaction in a water shower or steam canner.
27. Interaction jars for 20 minutes; increment time depending on the situation for your elevation.
28. RECIPE NOTES
29. The explanation you need a rimmed heating sheet is to forestall trickling juices ruining your oven. The explanation you line it with tin foil is to make tidy up simpler.
30. Make an honest effort not to stack the INGREDIENTS on the heating sheet or they will steam rather than broil.
31. TOMATOES: Plum tomato implies a paste, dry sort tomato like Roma, Amish Paste, San Marzano, and so forth
32. PEPPERS: Instead of jalapeno peppers, you could utilize another medium-hot pepper, for example, a green serrano. In the event that you need to diminish the heat for your crowd, supplant a few or the entirety of the jalapeno with green chime pepper yet don't go over the sum called for.
33. LIMES tip! Make your limes yield more squeeze by destroying them in the microwave, just until they feel warm outwardly. Around 30 seconds in a 1200 watt microwave; your mileage will

differ. However, you will get significantly more squeeze out of your limes (and lemons) with this stunt. On the off chance that you do this, 3 key limes might be sufficient. On the off chance that don't do this, you will presumably require 4 key lime.

11. Roasted Salsa Verde

Prep Time 45 minutes Cook Time 2 hours Total Time 2 hours 45 minutes

INGREDIENTS

- 2 kg tomatillos (4 lbs)
- 2 onions medium
- 2 jalapeno peppers
- 6 cloves garlic
- 125 ml lime juice (new. ½ cup/4 oz. Around 4 to 6 key limes)
- 25 g coriander (otherwise known as cilantro. Chopped new. ¼ cup/1 oz/4 tablespoons)
- 2 teaspoons salt (OR non-harsh, non-obfuscating salt sub)
- 1 teaspoon ground black pepper

INSTRUCTIONS

1. Get a large, rimmed preparing sheet and line it with tin foil.
2. Begin heating oven to 225 C/425 F.

3. Husk the tomatillos, and wash them. Try not to strip. Orchestrate on heating sheet, stem side down.
4. Wash the jalapenos, cut down the middle. Seed or not - dependent upon you. Spot cut side down on plate.
5. Try not to strip the onion. Cut each into wedges of four. Organize on heating sheet, strip sides up.
6. Strip the cloves of garlic. Add to plate.
7. Put plate in oven, prepare until garlic cloves are delicate - around 15 minutes.
8. Eliminate garlic, put in a food processor bowl.
9. Set plate back in oven, and prepare until onion is delicate - about an additional 15 minutes. Peppers and tomatillos ought to be beginning to burn a piece.
10. Eliminate plate from oven, and let remain to cool a piece.
11. Eliminate and dispose of stems and seeds from the peppers, add peppers to a food processor bowl.
12. Eliminate and dispose of skin from onion, add onion to food processor bowl.
13. Add tomatillos to food processor bowl. (Honestly, the tomatillos never get stripped.)
14. Master in food processor until smooth.
15. Put in a pot in any event 4 liters (quarts) in size.
16. Add every one of the excess INGREDIENTS .
17. Bring to a stew, at that point eliminate pot from heat.
18. Spoon hot sauce into heated jars, leaving 2 cm (½ inch) headspace.

19. Debubble, change headspace.
20. Wipe jar edges.
21. Put covers on.
22. Cycle in a water shower or steam canner.
23. Cycle jars for 20 minutes; increment time depending on the situation for your height.
24. RECIPE NOTES
25. The explanation you need a rimmed preparing sheet is to forestall trickling juices ruining your oven. The explanation you line it with tin foil is to make tidy up simpler.
26. Make an honest effort not to stack the INGREDIENTS on the preparing sheet or they will steam rather than cook.
27. TOMATILLOS: To be clear, they don't get stripped anytime.
28. ONIONS: We are leaving the strip on the onion only for the cooking part, so the strip can help shield the onion from drying out. The recipe says cut each into wedges of 8, however doing just 4 wedges forgets about less surface to dry/potentially consume in the oven. Utilize white or yellow onions.
29. PEPPERS: Instead of jalapeno peppers, you could utilize another medium-hot pepper, for example, a green serrano. On the off chance that you need to utilize different peppers, keep them green or yellow for the shading, and remember that the heaviness of two normal jalapenos, with stem and seeds in, will be 30 to 60 g (1 to 2 oz) consolidated, so close to that of elective pepper. On the off chance that you need to leave out all heat for your crowd, you could utilize a comparable load of green

ringer pepper or, you can just utilize 1 jalapeno to decrease the heat a piece. It's consistently protected to diminish the new pepper in salsas, you can't build it.
30. LIMES tip! Make your limes yield more squeeze by destroying them in the microwave, just until they feel warm outwardly. Around 30 seconds in a 1200 watt microwave; your mileage will differ. Yet, you will get significantly more squeeze out of your limes (and lemons) with this stunt. On the off chance that you do this, 4 key limes might be sufficient. In the event that don't do this, you will likely need 6 key limes. What's more, indeed, you could utilize packaged lime squeeze all things considered.

12. Tomatillo Green Salsa

Prep Time 45 minutes Cook Time 45 minutes Total Time 1 hour 30 minutes Yield 5 half-litre (US pint) jars Calories 18 kcal

INGREDIENTS

- 1 kg tomatillos (chopped. 5 cups/2.25 lbs. Estimated after prep)
- 200 g green chiles (stemmed, cultivated and finely chopped. 1 ½ cups/5 oz. Estimated after prep)
- 75 g jalapeno peppers (stemmed, cultivated and finely chopped. ½ cup/2 oz. Estimated after prep. 3 jalapenos)
- 700 g onion (finely chopped. 4 cups/25 oz. Estimated after prep)
- 6 cloves garlic (washed, stripped and finely chopped)
- 250 ml lime juice (packaged. 1 cup/8 oz. Or on the other hand same measure of packaged lemon juice.)
- 1 tablespoon ground cumin (optional)

- 3 tablespoons oregano (dried. optional)
- 1 tablespoon salt (OR non-unpleasant, non-obfuscating salt sub)
- 1 teaspoon ground black pepper

INSTRUCTIONS
1. Husk the tomatillos, wash well. Add to a pot.
2. Stem, seed and hack the peppers; add to the pot.
3. Strip, wash and hack the onion. Add to pot.
4. Strip and hack the garlic, add to pot.
5. Put pot on oven burner over high heat.
6. Heat to the point of boiling, blending as often as possible.
7. Lower to a stew and stew revealed for 20 minutes, mixing occasionally.
8. Scoop hot salsa into hot jars.
9. Leave 2 cm (½ inch) headspace.
10. Debubble, change headspace.
11. Wipe jar edges.
12. Put covers on.
13. Interaction in a water shower or steam canner.
14. Interaction jars for 15 minutes; increment time on a case by case basis for your height.
15. Honestly, you don't strip or seed the tomatillos (or green tomatoes, if using).
16. The recipe says "long green chiles", which would be the medium-hot cultivars advertised as "New Mexico Chiles" — you might need to strip those in the event that you use them as the skins can be intense. You can utilize other largish green chiles, and you will not have to strip them. In the event that you use poblano

for the green chile, you'll need three great measured new ones.
17. You don't have to strip the jalapenos.
18. You can really utilize any shade of chile, on the off chance that you couldn't care less about keeping the salsa all green.
19. For taking care of this amount of chile, you should wear plastic gloves.
20. Rather than 6 cloves of garlic, you can utilize 3 teaspoons of minced garlic from a without oil jug of minced garlic.
21. You could utilize a mix of the packaged lemon and packaged lime juice on the off chance that you wished. Try not to utilize vinegar all things considered — it's not as acidic.
22. Try not to change the extent of veg to acid. The lone safe changes you can make are the dry flavors. Try not to add any new cilantro; use rather one of the numerous other salsa recipes that do call for it.

13. Pico de gallo

Prep Time 1 hour 30 minutes Cook Time 15 minutes
Yield 4 x half-litre jars (US pint) Calories 8 kcal

INGREDIENTS
- 1 kg Roma tomatoes (2 lbs. Weight subsequent to eliminating seeds.)
- 1 onion (medium)
- 1 jalapeno peppers (large)
- 2 tablespoons coriander (otherwise known as cilantro. New, washed and chopped)
- 125 ml lime juice (packaged. ½ cup/4 oz)
- 1 teaspoon salt (OR non-harsh, non-blurring salt sub)

INSTRUCTIONS
1. Get a medium-sized sauce pot.
2. Wash, center, divide and seed the tomatoes. Cleave finely. Add to pot.
3. Strip the onion, cleave finely, add to pot.
4. Wash, stem, seed and cleave the jalapeno finely, add to pot.
5. Add all excess INGREDIENTS to pot.

6. Heat to the point of boiling.
7. Diminish heat to low, and let stew revealed for 3 minutes.
8. Spoon sauce into heated jars, leaving 2 cm (½ inch) headspace.
9. Debubble, change headspace.
10. Wipe jar edges.
11. Put covers on.
12. Interaction in a water shower or steam canner.
13. Cycle jars for 15 minutes; increment time on a case by case basis for your height.
14. RECIPE NOTES
15. You can utilize a food processor to do the hacking, or do it by hand with your #1 ordinary kitchen blade, or, you can go these consolidated through a food plant with a salsa connection set up.
16. All things considered, you don't strip the tomato. The super acidity here of all the lime juice deals with any stress over the strip here.
17. Try not to avoid the cultivating step. In the event that you leave the seeds and the gel sac around them in, you will get a runnier salsa. Likewise the seeds may add a dash of sharpness to certain individuals' preferences.
18. Individuals regularly report getting just 3 jars rather than the 4 you will, so be intellectually ready for a lower yield.

14. Salsa Roja

Prep Time 1 hour 30 minutes Cook Time 25 minutes
Yield 3 quarter-litre jars Calories 146 kcal

INGREDIENTS
- 600 g plum tomatoes (1 ¼ lbs. Weight before prep.)
- 1 onion (little. 40 g to 70 g/1 ½ oz to 2 ½ oz)
- 6 cloves garlic
- 6 ancho chiles (dried)
- 500 ml water (bubbling. 2 cups/16 oz)
- 4 tablespoons lime juice (new. 60 ml/2 oz)
- salt and pepper (optional)

INSTRUCTIONS
1. Start oven heating to 220 C (425 F/Gas mark 7.)
2. Wash tomatoes, center, cut down the middle and spot cut side up on large rimmed ungreased heating sheet.
3. Leave onion stripped, cut in fours, add to heating sheet skin sides down.
4. Strip garlic cloves, seal in a little piece of tin foil, add to preparing sheet.

5. Prepare until tomatoes and onion begin to get delicate, and brown a piece. Eliminate heating sheet from oven and let cool.
6. Heat an ungreased skillet (for example cast iron or a frying pan) until hot.
7. Flush dried chiles and wipe off.
8. Put the dried chiles in the container, and let each side toast for around 10 seconds, or until they simply begin to puff. (Try not to permit to singe.)
9. Put them in a bowl and cover with the bubbling water to mellow - around 15 to 20 minutes.
10. Eliminate strips on cooked veg and add put them all into a food processor bowl.
11. At the point when the chiles are delicate, channel however save water. Eliminate the stems, tear them open and wash them in the water to flush off the seeds. Add the chiles (not the water) to the food processor bowl .
12. Add lime juice to the food processor bowl.
13. Genius the combination in the food processor until smooth.
14. Whenever wanted, Ball says you may add a touch of the chile splashing water to thin the combination a piece. Dispose of the remainder of the water.
15. Whenever wanted, change taste with salt and pepper.
16. Put salsa in a skillet and reheat on oven OR put in microwave-safe container or bowl and zap until quite hot.
17. Spoon sauce into heated jars, leaving 2 cm (½ inch) headspace.
18. Debubble, change headspace.

19. Wipe jar edges.
20. Put covers on.
21. Cycle in a water shower or steam canner.
22. Interaction jars for 25 minutes; increment time depending on the situation for your elevation.
23. You will need around 100 g (3.5 oz) of ancho peppers. By and large, an ancho gauges 17 g (.6 oz)
24. Rather than the entire tomatoes, you could utilize 350 ml (12 oz 1 ½ cups) of squashed tomatoes. Cook simply the onion and garlic; add the squashed tomato to the food processor bowl at stage 10 above.
25. Salt utilized (optional) shouldn't pickle salt since we are not stressed over blurring here. Rather than salt, you may utilize a non-harsh salt sub.
26. There is no arrangement for canning larger-sized jars. Be that as it may, these size jars are typically the ideal recipe size at any rate.
27. You'll need around 2 key limes. Tip! To improve juice yield, destroy in microwave prior to slicing for 20 to 30 seconds relying upon strength of your microwave. Brain spurting hot juice when cutting into the lime thereafter.
28. The justification toasting the chiles is to awaken the flavor.
29. 'Salsa' signifies 'sauce' and 'roja' signifies 'red.

15. Roasted Tomato Guajillo Salsa

Prep Time 1 hour 30 minutes Cook Time 30 minutes Total Time 2 hours Yield 4 quarter-litre jars (½ pint / 250 ml / 8 oz) Calories 117 kcal

INGREDIENTS

- 1 kg plum tomatoes (2 lbs)
- 1 onion (medium)
- 4 cloves garlic
- 12 guajillo chile peppers (large dried. Around 100 g/around 3 oz in weight.)
- 500 ml water (bubbling. 2 cups/16 oz)
- 2 tablespoons vinegar (Either malt vinegar OR apple juice vinegar. 5% or higher)
- ½ teaspoon cumin (ground)
- ¼ teaspoon oregano (dried)
- salt and pepper (optional)

INSTRUCTIONS

1. Start oven heating to 220 C (425 F/gas mark 7.)

2. Wash tomatoes, center, cut down the middle and spot cut side up on large rimmed ungreased preparing sheet.
3. Leave onion stripped, cut in fours, add to heating sheet skin sides down.
4. Strip garlic cloves, seal in a little piece of tin foil, add to preparing sheet.
5. Heat until tomatoes and onion begin to get delicate, and brown somewhat: around 20 to 30 minutes. Eliminate preparing sheet from oven and let cool.
6. Heat an ungreased skillet (for example cast iron or a frying pan) until exceptionally hot.
7. Wash dried chiles and wipe off.
8. Put the dried chiles in the container, and let each side toast for around 10 seconds, or until they simply begin to puff. (Try not to permit to sear.)
9. Put them in a bowl and cover with the bubbling water to relax - around 15 to 20 minutes.
10. Eliminate strips on broiled veg and put them all into a food processor.
11. At the point when the chiles are delicate, eliminate the stems, tear them open and wash them in the water to flush off the seeds. Add the chiles to food processor.
12. Add to food processor the vinegar, the cumin and the oregano.
13. Star the combination in the food processor until smooth.
14. Whenever wanted, you may add a touch of the chile dousing water to thin it a piece. Dispose of the remainder of the water, or freeze for another utilization, for example, cooking rice

in. (Try not to add in excess of a piece to the salsa, or you may bring down its necessary safe acidity. Apologies, the recipe authors don't characterize what they mean by "a piece.")
15. Whenever wanted, change taste with salt (or salt sub) and pepper.
16. Put sauce in a skillet and reheat on oven OR put in microwave-safe container or bowl and zap until quite hot.
17. Scoop hot sauce into heated jars, leaving 2 cm (½ inch) headspace.
18. Debubble, change headspace.
19. Wipe jar edges.
20. Put covers on.
21. Cycle in a water shower or steam canner.
22. Cycle jars for 30 minutes; increment time on a case by case basis for your elevation.
23. RECIPE NOTES
24. There are generally around 4 Guajillo peppers for each 30 g/oz.
25. in the event that you can't get Guajillo peppers, utilize an identical measure of ancho peppers.
26. in the event that you can get Mexican oregano, you should utilize it.
27. Salt utilized (optional) shouldn't pickle salt.
28. There is no arrangement for canning larger-sized jars.
29. Subsequent to opening, store any extra sauce in the shrouded jar in the fridge for as long as about fourteen days. For longer term stockpiling than that, freeze the extra sauce or it will at last go rotten and ruin.

16. Green tomato salsa

Prep Time 45 minutes Cook Time 50 minutes Total Time 1 hour 35 minutes Yield 6 quarter-litre (½) jars Calories 12 kcal

INGREDIENTS
- 1.5 kg green tomatoes (estimated in the wake of stripping and hacking coarsely. Around 7 cups/12 medium/3 ¼ lbs)
- 250 g peppers (blended, like jalapeno, Habañero or Scotch hood peppers. ½ lb. Around 5 to 10.)
- 400 g onion (stripped and chopped. 2 cups/¾ lb. Around 2 large.)
- 2 cloves garlic (finely chopped)
- 125 ml lime juice (packaged. ½ cup/4 oz)
- 35 g coriander (otherwise known as cilantro. New, finely chopped. About ½ cup approximately stuffed. 1 oz)
- 2 teaspoons cumin (ground)
- 1 teaspoons oregano (dried)

- 1 teaspoons salt
- 1 teaspoons ground black pepper

INSTRUCTIONS
1. Wash the tomatoes. Whiten the tomatoes for around 60 seconds in bubbling water, at that point dive promptly into freezing water. Cut off and dispose of the strip. Cleave. Measure to make up amount determined in INGREDIENTS . Add tomato to a large pot. Wash and prep the pepper, onion and garlic, and add to same pot.
2. Add the lime juice.
3. Heat to the point of boiling.
4. Include the excess INGREDIENTS .
5. Lower heat and stew for 3 minutes.
6. Spoon into quarter-liter (½ US half quart) or half-liter (US half quart) jars.
7. Leave 2 cm (½ inch) headspace.
8. Debubble, change headspace.
9. Wipe jar edges.
10. Put covers on.
11. Cycle in a water shower or steam canner.
12. Cycle either size jar for 20 minutes; increment time on a case by case basis for your height.
13. Best after in any event a month of jar time.

17. Peach Salsa

Prep Time 1 hour Cook Time 45 minutes Total Time 1 hour 45 minutes Yield 8 x quarter-litre jars (½ pint / 8 oz) Calories 11 kcal

INGREDIENTS
- 125 ml white vinegar (5 % or more grounded. ½ cup/4 oz)
- 1 kg peaches (About 6 cups chopped in largish parts/2 lbs. Estimated in the wake of being stripped and pitted; 6 medium before prep.)
- 200 g onion (finely chopped. 1 ¼ cups/7 oz)
- 4 jalapeno peppers (around 100 g/3 oz entire prior to cultivating and slashing)
- 1 red ringer pepper (around 200 g/7 oz entire prior to cultivating and slashing. Around 150 g/5 oz in the wake of cultivating and cleaving)
- 40 g coriander (also known as cilantro. New, finely chopped. About ½ cup, approximately stuffed, 1.5 oz.)
- 1 clove garlic (minced)
- 1 ½ teaspoons cumin (ground)
- ½ teaspoon cayenne pepper

- 2 tablespoons nectar
- 2 tablespoons lime juice (packaged or new. Optional, for flavor)

INSTRUCTIONS
1. Put vinegar in large pot.
2. Prep peaches, mixing pieces into vinegar in pot as you go to forestall browning.
3. Prep and add remaining INGREDIENTS to pot.
4. Blend INGREDIENTS in pot, heat to the point of boiling, at that point lower to a stew revealed for 5 to 10 minutes, until the combination thickens however you would prefer, remembering that it will thicken all the more once cold so don't attempt to bubble it strong. Mix much of the time to forestall consuming.
5. Spoon into your decision of the accompanying jar sizes: 125 ml (4 oz) jars or ¼ liter (½ US half quart/8 oz/250 ml) jars.
6. Leave 2 cm (½ inch) headspace paying little heed to jar size.
7. Debubble, change headspace.
8. Wipe jar edges.
9. Put tops on.
10. Interaction in a water shower or steam canner.
11. Interaction either size jar for 15 minutes; increment time on a case by case basis for your height.
12. Best after at any rate a month of jar time.
13. RECIPE NOTES
14. To strip the peaches: wash the peaches, and plunge them in a pot of bubbling water for about a moment, until the skins release. At

that point plunge in cool water, strip the skin off, and eliminate pit. Hack peach into pieces around 2 to 3 cm (1 inch) for a stout salsa; somewhat more modest is likewise fine in the event that you wish. Mix into vinegar in pot as you go to forestall browning.

15. In the event that you need to make this unavailable, you can use rather 1 liter (4 cups) of depleted canned peach cuts or pieces. You'll have to purchase around 2 x 800 ml/28 oz tins. Measure them out, at that point hack them as needed by recipe. Or then again, you could utilize frozen. Measure out frozen, at that point defrost. Remember for the recipe any juice from them as they defrost.
16. You can cleave the peach in a food processor for decent even pieces, however give it a short prodigy: you are making salsa here, not child pablum, and a second excessively long and you could wind up with moosh.
17. Rather than white vinegar, you could utilize apple juice vinegar (5% or more grounded)
18. The nectar is only there to balance the flavor, you can exclude whenever wanted.
19. The lime juice is only an expansion for flavor. Rather than lime juice, you could utilize packaged lemon squeeze, or overlook.
20. You can securely build the heat by leaving a portion of the jalapeno seed in, or by using an equivalent measure of more sweltering peppers, or with a couple of portions of dried chile piece, or, with a couple of sprinkles of a hot sauce.

21. How long of stewing it needs precisely to thicken will rely upon how delicious the peaches were.
22. Not long prior to packaging, you may wish to take a little spoonful, put away briefly, and taste (you can't sincerely taste the flavors when it is extremely hot.) And at that point, whenever wanted, season with a touch of salt or salt sub.

18. Smoky Sour Cherry Tequila Salsa

Prep Time 1 hour Cook Time 30 minutes Total Time 1 hour 30 minutes Yield 4 x half-litre jars (US pint) Calories 97 kcal

INGREDIENTS
- 300 g onion (diced. 2 cups/10 oz. Estimated after prep)
- 1 clove garlic (washed, stripped and minced)
- 4 tablespoons lime juice (newly pressed. ¼ cup/2 oz/60 ml)
- 50 g coriander (otherwise known as cilantro. Chopped new. ½ cup/2 oz)
- 2 chipotle chiles (from an adobo sauce tin)
- 1 serrano pepper (little red. 10 g/.3 oz)
- 2 kg sharp cherries (new. 4 lb/13 cups. Estimated after prep)
- 125 g brown sugar (½ cup immovably stuffed/4 oz) OR 1 teaspoon fluid stevia
- 4 tablespoons tequila (¼ cup/2 oz/60 ml)
- 1 ½ teaspoons salt (OR non-blurring, non-unpleasant salt sub)

- ½ teaspoon ground black pepper

INSTRUCTIONS
1. Strip and dice the onion, put away.
2. Strip and mince the garlic, add to the onion.
3. Press the lime juice, put away.
4. Wash and cleave the coriander, put away.
5. Mince the two chipotle peppers, put away in a little dish.
6. Seed and mince the serrano pepper, add to the chipotle pepper.
7. Wash the cherries. Stem and pit them, setting them in acidulated water as you work to forestall browning.
8. In a large non-responsive pot (pure or plated), put the onion, garlic, sugar OR fluid stevia and lime juice.
9. Turn the burner onto medium heat, and cook for 5 minutes, blending frequently.
10. Add the depleted cherries, the new coriander, and the two chopped up peppers.
11. Cook for an additional 5 minutes, blending regularly.
12. Add the tequila, salt OR salt sub and pepper.
13. Heat back to the point of boiling.
14. Eliminate from heat.
15. Pack hot into ¼ liter (½ US half quart) jars or ½ liter (US half quart) jars.
16. Leave 2 cm (½ inch) headspace.
17. Debubble, change headspace.
18. Wipe jar edges.
19. Put tops on.
20. Interaction in a water shower or steam canner.

21. Interaction either size jar for 15 minutes. Increment time depending on the situation for your height.
22. Best after at any rate a month of jar time.
23. RECIPE NOTES
24. For this recipe, it truly is ideal to do all veg prep ahead of time on the grounds that once you start the cooking there will be no an ideal opportunity for prep in the middle of stages.
25. Rather than a serrano pepper, you can utilize another of a similar size or weight.

19.   Mild Salsa

Prep Time 1 hour Cook Time 45 minutes Total Time 1 hour 45 minutes Yield 12 x quarter-litre (US ½ pint / 250 ml) jars

INGREDIENTS
- 1.5 kg paste tomatoes (otherwise known as plum, Roma, and so on Coarsely chopped. Estimated after prep. Around 3 pounds/6 cups.)
- 300 g onion (stripped, finely chopped. 2 cups/10 oz. Estimated after prep.)
- 1 kg chime pepper (cultivated, finely chopped. 7 cups/2 lbs. Estimated after prep.)
- 250 ml lemon juice (packaged. 1 cup/8 oz)
- 125 ml lime juice (packaged. ½ cup/4 oz)
- 1 tablespoon salt
- 1 teaspoon cumin (dried)
- 1 teaspoon oregano (dried)
- 1 ½ teaspoons chile chips (optional)

INSTRUCTIONS

1. Strip the tomatoes. This is truly simple done by washing the tomatoes, at that point bubbling them for 1 to 3 to 5 minutes (contingent upon the tomatoes) in steaming hot water, at that point diving them into a skillet, sink or large bowl of freezing water. The skins will pull off without any problem.
2. Hack tomato coarsely into around 2 cm (½ inch) pieces and add to large pot.
3. Prep onion (food processor with heartbeat button is fine) and add to pot.
4. Wash the peppers, stem and seed them, at that point slash finely (food processor with heartbeat button is fine) and add to pot.
5. Add lemon and lime juice to pot.
6. Add flavors (starting from the salt to the chile chip) to the pot.
7. Put pot on the burner and heat to the point of boiling, mixing oftentimes to keep away from searing on base.
8. At the point when it hits a bubble, diminish heat and let stew for 3 minutes, blending a couple of times.
9. Spoon into quarter-liter (½ US half quart) or half-liter (US half quart) jars.
10. Leave 2 cm (½ inch) headspace.
11. Debubble, change headspace.
12. Wipe jar edges.
13. Put tops on.
14. Interaction in a water shower or steam canner.
15. Interaction either size jar for 15 minutes; increment time depending on the situation for your height.
16. Best after at any rate a month of jar time.

17. Instructions to water shower measure.
18. Step by step instructions to steam can.
19. At the point when water-shower canning or steam canning, you should change the handling time for your height.
20. RECIPE NOTES
21. For the pepper, you could trade out some sweet pepper and trade in an equivalent measure of peppier pepper.
22. Try not to add any new spices for canning, whatever amount of you need to. Add at season of serving. That way they'll be really new, in any case.
23. You are stripping the tomatoes to diminish the bacterial burden going into the canner.
24. Indeed, the lemon and lime juices should be packaged, to guarantee that an ensured acidity is being utilized. See Ball All New on the off chance that you like to make new squeeze salsas.
25. On the off chance that you need to expand the heat do as such by using dried chile chip.
26. You are permitted to increment/decline pungency/sweetness to taste. In this manner:
27. You can add more salt, to taste.
28. Rather than the salt, you can utilize a non-severe, non-obfuscating salt sub. We have discovered Herbamare Sodium-Free performs well around there.
29. In the event that you discover the tomatoes not exactly sweet enough, to balance the taste you can add a couple of tablespoons of sugar, or, Splenda, or fluid stevia ¼ teaspoon at a time.

Conclusion

I would like to thank you for choosing this book. These recipes will help you in pressure canning different kind of salsa in a better and healthy way. Hope you try and appreciate.
Good luck!